The Allen Book of
RIDING

by Carolyn Henderson and Jennifer Bell

Starting Out

The best place to learn how to ride is at a good riding school, because you will find trained instructors and suitable ponies. It is easier and safer to learn this way than on a friend's pony.

The pony you are given for your early lessons will be quiet and reliable, he will be used to beginners and will not get upset if you make a mistake.

Ponies come in lots of different colours, from bay (brown with black mane, tail and the lower part of the legs) to skewbald (brown and white) and piebald (black and white.) Grey ponies usually get lighter as they grow older and a white pony is officially always grey.

There are many breeds of ponies, ranging from tiny Shetlands to larger ones such as New Forest and Connemara, and many ponies are of mixed breeding.

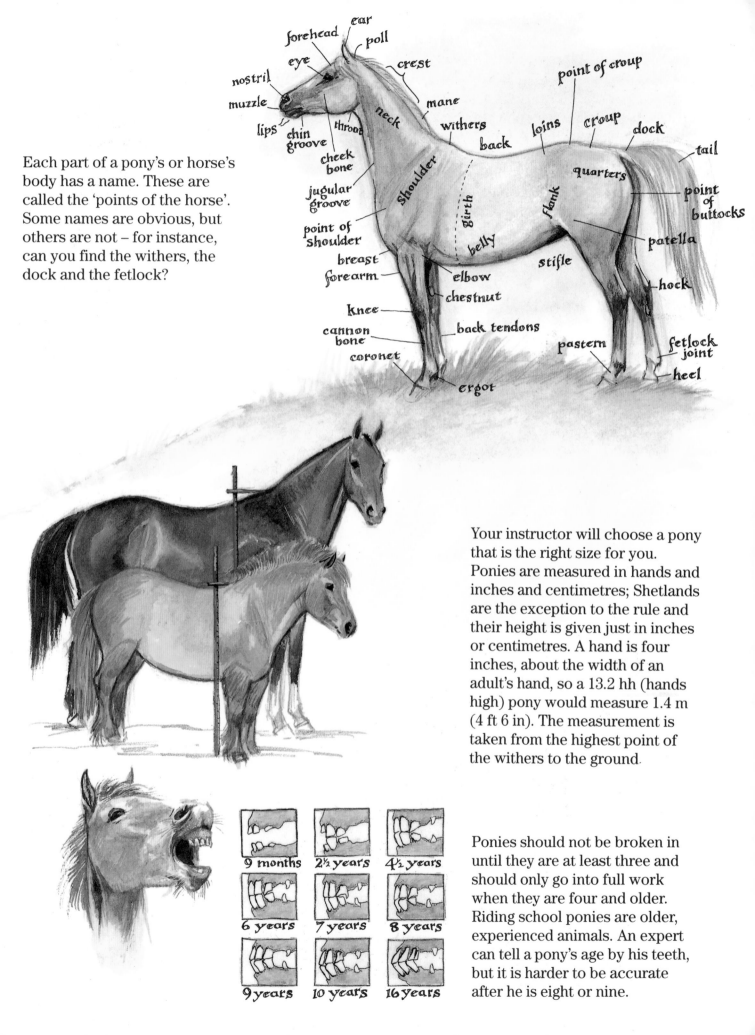

Each part of a pony's or horse's body has a name. These are called the 'points of the horse'. Some names are obvious, but others are not – for instance, can you find the withers, the dock and the fetlock?

Points of the horse labels: ear, forehead, poll, eye, crest, nostril, muzzle, mane, lips, chin groove, throat, neck, withers, point of croup, loins, croup, dock, tail, back, cheek bone, quarters, point of buttocks, jugular groove, shoulder, girth, flank, patella, point of shoulder, breast, belly, stifle, hock, forearm, elbow, chestnut, knee, back tendons, pastern, fetlock joint, cannon bone, heel, coronet, ergot

Your instructor will choose a pony that is the right size for you. Ponies are measured in hands and inches and centimetres; Shetlands are the exception to the rule and their height is given just in inches or centimetres. A hand is four inches, about the width of an adult's hand, so a 13.2 hh (hands high) pony would measure 1.4 m (4 ft 6 in). The measurement is taken from the highest point of the withers to the ground.

9 months · 2½ years · 4½ years
6 years · 7 years · 8 years
9 years · 10 years · 16 years

Ponies should not be broken in until they are at least three and should only go into full work when they are four and older. Riding school ponies are older, experienced animals. An expert can tell a pony's age by his teeth, but it is harder to be accurate after he is eight or nine.

What to Wear

Riders at shows and other competitions look very smart in their formal clothes, but you do not need to buy everything at once; a hat or skull cap, safe footwear and comfortable clothes that will not rub or pinch are all you need to start. A good saddler will help you choose headgear to British Standards, which will carry a kitemark symbol. Never buy a secondhand hat because it may have been damaged in a fall.

Leather jodhpur boots or long rubber boots are most comfortable, but you can wear shoes as long as they have a small heel and no buckles to catch on the stirrups. Wellington boots are all right if they have a small heel and soles without ridges (which could trap the stirrup irons). Trainers without heels are dangerous because your foot could slide right through the stirrup. Riding boots with protective steel toecaps are the safest of all because they may prevent injury if a pony stands on your foot.

Later on you will want a pair of jodhpurs, but comfortable jeans, leggings or tracksuit bottoms will do at first.

Gloves stop your hands from being rubbed. Look for cotton or woolly ones with rubber 'pimples' on the palm to give a secure grip.

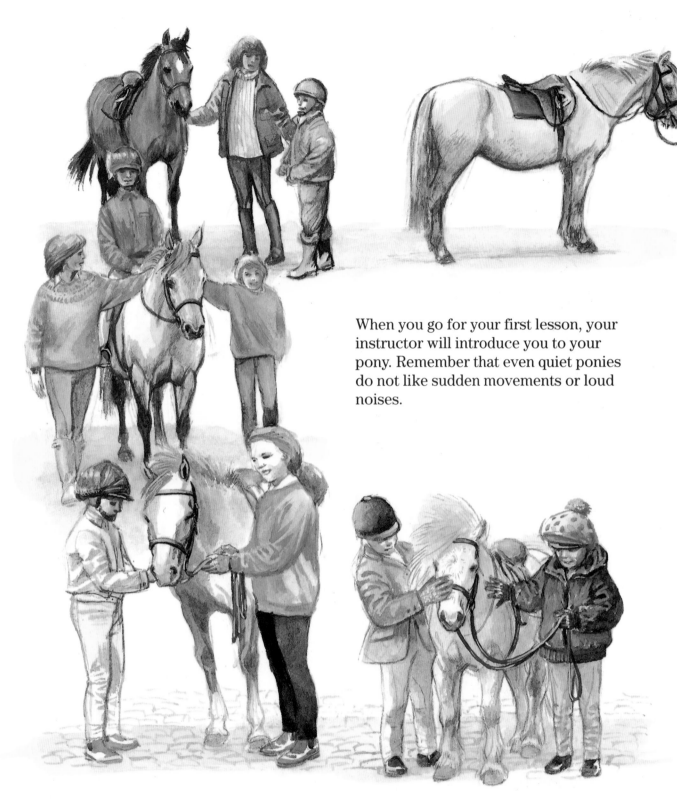

When you go for your first lesson, your instructor will introduce you to your pony. Remember that even quiet ponies do not like sudden movements or loud noises.

Riding school ponies should not kick or bite. They may not take much notice of being stroked or patted, however, because they are handled and ridden by so many people that they take such attention for granted. But be careful not to get your toes trodden on – he will not do it on purpose, but it still hurts!

You may feel a little nervous before your first lesson . . . especially when you see people your age or younger riding confidently. Your confidence will soon grow, and after about a year of weekly lessons you will be able to walk, trot and canter and jump small fences.

Preparations

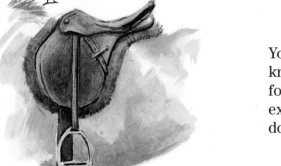

Your pony will wear a saddle and bridle – this is known as his tack. He should also wear a neckstrap for you to hold if you lose your balance or need extra confidence. Holding the neckstrap means you do not pull on the reins and hurt the pony's mouth.

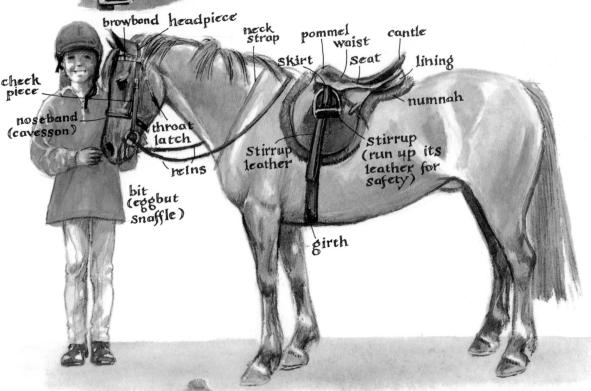

browband   headpiece   neck strap   pommel   cantle

waist

skirt   seat   lining

cheek piece

numnah

noseband (cavesson)

throat latch

stirrup (run up its leather for safety)

reins

stirrup leather

bit (eggbut snaffle)

girth

The saddle and bridle parts all have different names. This bridle has an eggbutt snaffle bit and a cavesson noseband, but there are many different kinds.

Your instructor will make sure that your pony's tack fits correctly. It is important that the stirrup irons are the right size for your feet: if they are too small, your foot could get trapped and if they are too large, it could slip right through. The stirrup irons should be an inch wider than the widest part of your boot.

Getting on and off the pony – mounting and dismounting – is easy once you have had some practice. Before you mount, check that the girth is tight enough to prevent the saddle slipping round when your weight is in the stirrup. It is usual to mount and dismount from the near (left) side, though you should practise from the off (right) side too in case you ever find yourself in a position where you only have room to mount on this side.

Hold the reins in your left hand and spread your fingers across the pony's neck, just in front of the withers. The reins should be short enough to stop him walking off.

Hold the stirrup iron by the side farthest away from you and turn it towards you. This turns the stirrup leather so that it will not pinch your leg when you are in the saddle.

Facing the pony's hindquarters, put your left foot in the stirrup. If he walks off, you are in the best position to stop him or mount quickly, but if you face his head and he moves, you could be left hopping about with very little control.

Swivel round so that you face the pony. Use your left hand to balance yourself and rest your right hand lightly across the saddle seat. Push off from your right foot – your weight will now be taken on the left foot, in the stirrup. Keep your left toe down so you do not prod the pony in the stomach and move your right hand across so it rests on the top of the saddle flap.

Swing your right leg over the saddle, settle lightly on his back and slip your right foot into the stirrup iron. Take up the reins in both hands and you are nearly ready to ride!

Getting On

dismounting

When you want to dismount, take both feet out the stirrups and hold the reins in your left hand. Rest your left hand lightly in front of the withers and your right one on the front of the saddle. Then swing your right leg over the back of the saddle, being careful not to catch the pony with your toe, and land on both feet.

Mounting and dismounting become easy with practice. You may be asked to use a mounting block, which helps prevent the saddle being pulled over. Another method is to have a leg-up, but the person helping you must know what he or she is doing! If you are being legged up, stand facing the pony's side and put the reins in your left hand. Rest your left hand in front of the withers and your right hand on the back of the saddle. Bend your left leg at the knee so that your helper can support you. On the count of three, push off from your right foot – the helper should lift at the same time so that you can swing your right leg over the pony's back and settle quietly in the saddle.

getting a leg~up

too long

too short

right

holding the reins correctly

Your stirrups need to be adjusted to the correct length. At first, your instructor will do this for you, but later you will learn to do it yourself. If the stirrup leathers are too long, you will feel insecure and your legs will hang down straight instead of at the correct angle. If they are too short, you will feel like a jockey, which will again make you too insecure for ordinary riding. The stirrup irons should be under the broadest part of your feet and your heels should be level or slightly down: do not force them down, but make sure they are not higher than your toes.

Hold the reins in both hands. They should run between your little and third finger and out between your thumb and first finger. Keep your thumbs on top and your elbows bent: this will help you feel the pony's mouth without pulling. The reins should be short enough so that your hands are just above the pony's withers without any loops hanging down.

Imagine you are holding a little bird in each hand. You have to hold them tightly enough to prevent them flying away, but not so tightly that they are uncomfortable.

Sitting correctly is not just someone's idea of what looks nice: the right position keeps you in balance and helps you to give clear signals to your pony.

Your instructor will show you how to sit in the centre of the saddle and adjust your balance so that you are comfortable but secure.

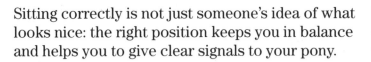

Your legs should rest round the pony's sides, but you do not need to grip to hold on. If you find it hard not to grip, take both feet out the stirrups, hold the front of the saddle and lift your legs so that your knees are above the pommel. Then open your legs to the side and let them drop down gently – this will stretch your muscles so that when you put your feet back in the stirrups, your legs rest comfortably.

Ideally, someone looking at you from the side should be able to draw an imaginary straight line from your ear, down to your elbow, hip and heel to the ground. There should be another imaginary straight line from the pony's bit rings to your elbow.

line through elbow, hand, along rein to the bit

From the back, you should look as if you are sitting straight – not collapsed to one side or the other.

line through heel, hip, shoulder to ear

At first this may not seem the most comfortable way to sit on a pony, but once you get used to it you will realise that it helps you to feel how he moves and give him clear signals. It also makes it easier for him to adjust his balance and carry your weight. Imagine you are carrying a heavy rucksack – if you balance it correctly on your back, the load is easy to bear, but if you get it in the wrong position, it becomes very difficult.

oo-er

umphh

erggghh

On the Lunge

lead rein

Your first lessons will be on the lungeing rein or lead rein, so the instructor can control the pony and you can concentrate on what you are being told. A lunge rein is a long rein and the pony is sent in big circles round the instructor; a lead rein is a shorter rein that the instructor holds while walking beside you.

lunge rein

You need to tell your pony how to stop, start and change gait. This is done with signals called the aids, e.g. closing your legs against his side or closing your fingers round the reins. To ask him to walk on, make sure you have a light but not strong feel (contact) on the reins, look ahead and close your legs round his sides. If he does not respond immediately (and some ponies are better at this than others) stop squeezing for a couple of seconds and then squeeze a bit harder.

To stop, sit up straight and close your fingers on the reins, but try not to pull back on the reins. As soon as the pony slows down, relax them. Whatever signal you give, it is important to stop as soon as the pony obeys so he knows he has done what is wanted. If he does not obey immediately, relax your fingers, then squeeze again; some ponies are more sensitive than others.

The walk is slow and comfortable and you will have time to think about your balance. Once you know how you should sit, imagine yourself riding this way. If you can picture it in your mind, it will come more easily.

You will not need to think about turning while you are on the lunge, but steering is important when your instructor lets you ride alone. Look in the direction you want to go and squeeze the rein on that side in a give and take motion: squeeze the left rein to go left and the right one to go right. At the same time, nudge the pony's side with your leg – nudge with the left leg when you turn left and the right leg when you turn right.

Trotting

Trotting feels very different from walking and you will probably find it easier to hold the front of the saddle as you get used to this new gait.

When you want to trot, shorten your reins a little; hold both reins in the right hand while you slide your left hand farther down the left rein, then shorten the right rein in the same way. Look ahead and close your legs round the pony's side. When you are on the lunge, your instructor may help by using her voice – ponies soon learn to walk, trot, canter and halt on command. If you hold the front of the saddle, make sure your reins are long enough to prevent you catching the pony in the mouth. As he starts to trot, try and absorb the movement through your body. You need to be relaxed but not floppy or stiff, so your muscles need to be firm enough to support you but not so tight that you bump up and down.

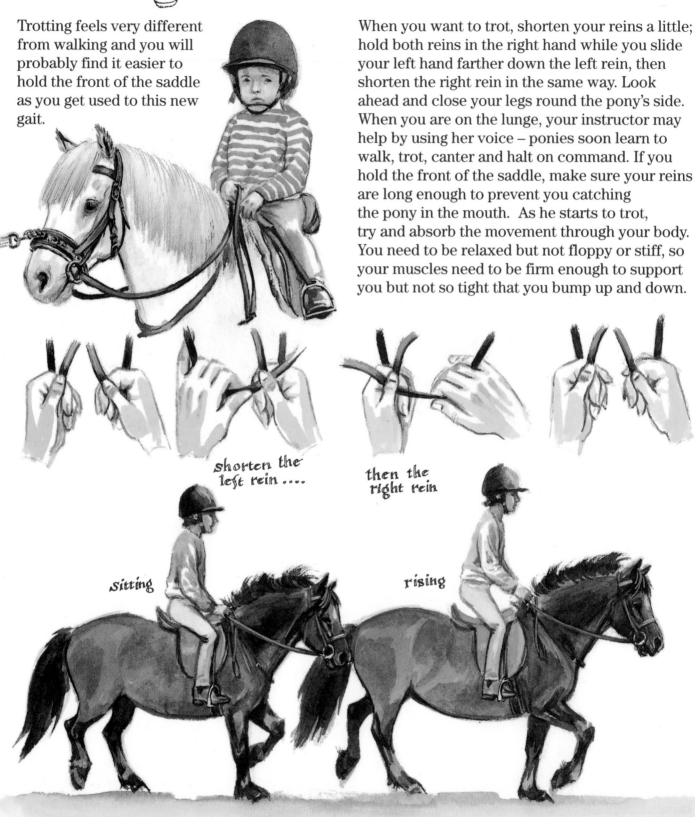

shorten the left rein ....

then the right rein

sitting

rising

Once you know what trotting feels like, you can learn to do rising trot (called posting in America). Here the rider moves up and down in perfect time with the pony. Once you have the knack, you will find it very comfortable. You do not need to stand up and down in the stirrups – let the pony's trot push you out, then sink back down. Your upper body should lean very slightly forwards so that you feel you are rising over the pommel of the saddle.

walk ....

.... to trot ...

sitting on the left diagonal

sitting on the right diagonal

In walk, the pony moves in a 1-2-3-4 rhythm. In trot, his legs move in diagonal pairs (near fore and off hind, then off fore and near hind) and you can count 1-2, 1-2 to the rhythm.

Once you are confident and comfortable, you can learn to rise on different diagonals and make it easier for the pony to carry you, in the same way that carrying a heavy bag is easier if you change it from one hand to the other.

sitting trot

Trotting on the left diagonal means you sit as his near fore comes to the ground; on the right diagonal, you sit as his off fore comes down. With practice, you can feel which diagonal you are on without looking – if you trot in a straight line for long periods, change your diagonal every now and again to make it easier for the pony.

Cantering

As you become more confident, your instructor will let you ride on your own in walk and trot as well as on the lunge. When you can stop, start and steer the pony and stay in balance with his movement, you will learn how to canter. The canter has a 1-2-3 rhythm and although it is faster than the trot, it is controlled and comfortable. Watch a pony cantering and you will see that one front leg always takes a longer stride than the other one; this is called the leading leg, whether it is the near fore or the off fore.

You sit to the canter and absorb the movement through your body. This takes practice and it may be easier if you hold the front of the saddle at first, as you did when learning to trot. Your instructor may get the pony to canter a big circle on the lunge so that you can get used to the feel of this new gait.

Now you can ask for canter. Ask in a corner of the school rather than on a straight line – if the pony is bent through his body he will find it easier to understand your aids because he will be in a natural position to move off correctly into canter.

If you canter on the left rein, the near fore should be the leading leg. If you canter on the right rein, the off fore should lead. So whatever way you are going, the leading leg is nearest the centre of the school. Leading with the inside leg helps keep the pony better balanced.

cantering on the lunge

To canter on the left rein, trot down the long side of the school going anti-clockwise. Just before you get to the corner, sit to the trot and feel the left rein to bend the pony round the corner. This also helps to warn him that he is going to be asked to do something different. Nudge your left leg on the girth and brush your right leg back slightly behind the girth; using both legs in this way helps keep the pony balanced and he will have been taught to understand these signals to move up to canter. As he goes into canter, think about sitting up and 'giving' the reins slightly – you should still have a light contact, but he will need to stretch his neck a little more than in trot.

cantering on the left rein

cantering on the right rein

skull cap and back protector for safety

flash noseband

running martingale for extra control

protective boots

a strong pony at the gallop

To canter on the right rein, trot to the corner going clockwise round the school. Feel the right rein, nudge your right leg on the girth and brush your left leg back.

A very fast canter is called a gallop, but you will only be able to try this when you are more experienced and can ride outside – you need plenty of room and to be able to see a long way ahead to gallop safely.

When galloping, bend forwards from the hips and take your weight off the saddle and down through your thighs and legs. Your reins must be short enough to maintain control and if the pony tries to go faster than you want, you should check him with a 'give and take' on the reins.

Exercises 1

Exercises to help you find and develop your balance are fun to do and will assist you to feel more comfortable and secure when you ride. Some can be done on the pony, but others are designed for you to do on your own. You can practise them at any time. Start with this one to loosen up your muscles before you ride. Raise your hands above your head, hold for a few seconds then let them drop.

Imagine your arms are made of jelly as they hang by your sides. Wiggle them so that the movement goes all the way from your shoulders, through your wrists and out through your fingers.

Shrug your shoulders as high as you can: imagine you are trying to touch your ears. Hold for a count of two, then let them drop.

stretching ~ up exercise

wiggling fingers

shrugging shoulders

Skipping is a good way to get fit for riding. Wear comfortable, well-fitting trainers to ensure your feet and ankles are supported and there is less risk of blisters. Start off gradually and build up to longer periods – think about setting up an easy rhythm as you skip.

Swimming and cycling are also good activities for riders. They help you build up your stamina and keep your arm and leg muscles toned up. When you cycle, pick a safe spot and cycle standing up rather than sitting on the seat for short periods.

skipping

cycling

leg strengthening

This exercise is a hard one, so always do your loosening-up session first and practise it for short periods to start with! Stand about 30 cms (1 ft) away from a wall, lean back against it and slide down until you are in a sitting position. Stay there for as long as you feel comfortable – which will probably be half a minute at first – then ease yourself into a standing position again.

Exercises 2

Your instructor will choose a very quiet pony when teaching you exercises in the saddle, and will hold him so that you do not have to worry about keeping him under control. Start by doing some of the loosening up exercises you practised on the ground: raise and drop your arms, wiggle them and shrug your shoulders.

Take both feet out of the stirrups, hold the front of the saddle with one hand and bring your knees up and together in front. Then take your legs out to the side and let them drop gently by the pony's side. Can you feel how your muscles have stretched? This helps you keep a secure and balanced position without gripping.

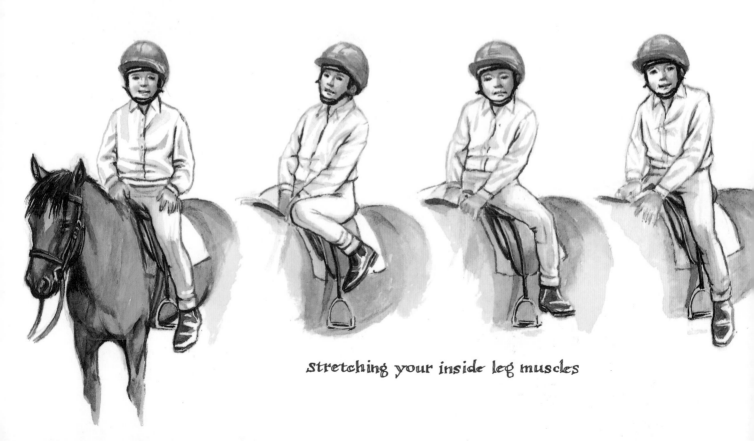

stretching your inside leg muscles

aeroplane exercise

Now try the aeroplane exercise. Put your feet back in the stirrups and stretch out both arms until they are level with your shoulders, as if they were the wings of an aeroplane. Keep your legs and hips steady while you swing your upper body round: one hand will point to the pony's tail and the other along his neck. Next, swing your upper body round to the other side in a mirror image of the first exercise. This will help keep your back and waist supple.

The next exercise is sometimes called bowing to the moon, but your instructor may know other names for it. It needs a pony who is especially quiet and it is not a good idea to do it on a day when there are lots of flies around because even the quietest pony may toss his head to get rid of them and bang you in the face without meaning to. Keep your hips and legs in the correct position and lean forwards so that your chin nearly touches the pony's mane. Stretch both arms out to the side, as you did with the aeroplane exercise, and go back to a sitting position. This helps you keep your weight down through your heels, because only by doing this will you be able to sit up easily.

bowing to the moon

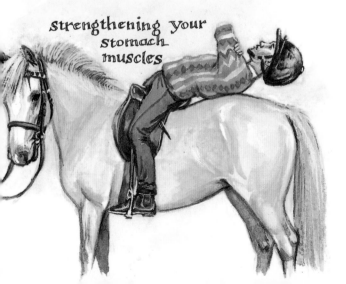

strengthening your stomach muscles

This exercise is the second part of bowing to the moon. Fold your arms and lean back slowly until your shoulders rest on the pony, keeping your lower body and legs in the correct position. Now sit up again. Notice the pull on your stomach muscles, this exercise helps to strengthen them.

Exercises 3

The round-the-world exercise helps keep you supple and agile. Take your feet out of the stirrups and cross the irons over the pony's withers, in front of the saddle – this keeps the irons out of the way and prevents them from banging your legs or the pony's sides. Swing your right leg over the pony's withers so that you are sitting 'side-saddle'. Then swing your left leg over the saddle (being careful not to bang or kick the pony) so you are facing his tail. Swing your right leg over so that you are sitting 'side saddle' on the opposite side, then pass your left leg over the withers to bring you back to the correct position.

Round-the-world exercise

riding without stirrups

stirrups crossed over

Riding without stirrups, usually on the lunge to start with, is an excellent way of establishing a relaxed but secure position. All riders should do this regularly, even experienced ones. As your confidence increases, you can ride without stirrups off the lunge, but, to be safe, make sure you are in a school or enclosed area.

This rider is enjoying an advanced exercise through a small grid of jumps, riding with crossed stirrups. It will help her develop a balanced position, but although it is not as difficult as it looks it should only be tried when your instructor is there to help you.

Riding bareback on a comfortable pony, in an enclosed area, is an enjoyable way of developing your sense of balance. Make sure the pony has a neckstrap for you to hold on to if you need it – and, again, make sure your instructor is with you.

riding bareback

You will find that practising exercises like these helps you to sit in a correct position, which in turn makes you better balanced and able to give clear aids to your pony. Keep a picture in your mind of how you should be sitting and it will start to become second nature.

Going for a Hack

Once you can walk, trot and canter off the lunge and can control your pony confidently, you will be able to ride out. This is often called 'hacking' or 'going for a hack' and most ponies enjoy it, because it gives them a change of scene. You will enjoy it too, but will have to concentrate on your riding just as much as you do in the school. Off-road tracks called bridleways or bridlepaths are the nicest and safest places to hack and your instructor may be able to take you along these if you have some in the area. Horses are not allowed on footpaths unless the landowner gives special permission.

Walkers and cyclists are also allowed to use bridlepaths, so be careful. Only canter if the ground is safe and you will not do any damage; if it is too hard, it will jar the pony's limbs and if it is too wet, he will cut it up with his hooves and may slip.

Even if the ground is good, you should only canter if you can see a long way ahead and can be sure you are not going to run into people coming from the other direction. Always pass other riders or cyclists at walk and watch out for hazards such as loose dogs and farm vehicles.

If bridleways go through fields with sheep or cattle in them, walk through: your pony may be as curious or nervous about them as they are of him, so be careful. Having ridden through gateways, shut any gates that were closed when you reached them: a good rider on a well-schooled pony who has been trained to cope with gate opening can sometimes do this from the saddle, but you will often have to dismount.

Most people have to ride on the roads at least some of the time, though you should never ride on roads in the dark. Ride on the left and make sure you can be seen. It is a good idea to wear a reflective, fluorescent belt or tabard, especially if the weather is dull or it is raining. Legbands in the same material are available for ponies, and riders can also wear flashing lights that clip on to boots or belts. There should always be experienced riders at the front and rear of a ride. Keep one pony's length between you and the pony in front.

Considerate drivers will slow down. Always thank them, but do not take a hand off the reins to signal your thanks unless you are sure it is safe to do so. A nod and a smile get the message across.

Do not move out into the road to change direction or go round an obstruction unless you have looked in front and behind to check that it is safe. Use hand signals to tell drivers what you intend to do. Look, signal and move out when it is safe.

Tacking Up

As part of the preparation for your lesson, you will learn to put on and take off your pony's saddle and bridle (tack). This is called tacking up and untacking. To put on a bridle, stand next to the pony's head on the nearside, facing forwards. Pass the reins over his head and hold the bridle in your right hand, about halfway down the cheekpieces. Support the bit in your left hand and ease it gently into his mouth, being careful not to bang his teeth. If he will not open his mouth, try pressing on the gums in the gap where the bit goes, or tickle his tongue. As the bit slides in, slip the headpiece gently over his head and guide his ears through the gap between headpiece and browband. Fasten the throatlatch (pronounced throatlash) so that you can fit a hand's width between it and the pony's face and fasten the noseband so that you can slip two fingers between the noseband and the pony's nose.

putting on a bridle

Sometimes you may have to tack up a pony who is tied up outside. Put the reins over his head, then undo the headcollar and fasten it round his neck – if he tries to walk off while you are unfastening the headcollar the reins give you a certain amount of control. Put on the bridle as before, and if he is to stay tied up for a few minutes either twist the reins and fasten them through a loosely secured throatlatch or (if they are long enough to give him enough freedom) put them behind the stirrup irons. Fasten the headcollar over the bridle, ensuring that it does not pinch the bit against the pony's face.

twine linking lead rope and ring

tacked-up pony safely tied up

Make sure the stirrups are run up the leathers and the girth is folded over the seat before you put on the saddle. Place it gently on the pony's back, farther forwards than it should lie, then slide it back so that the flaps lie behind his shoulders. This ensures that the coat hairs lie flat and he stays comfortable. If the pony wears a numnah, make sure it is pulled up into the gullet of the saddle so it does not press down on the withers or back.

Ensure that the girth is not twisted as it passes round the pony's belly and fasten it loosely at first. Tighten it gradually: some ponies blow out their stomachs to begin with. It often helps to walk the pony for a few steps before tightening the girth.

To remove a bridle, buckle a headcollar round the pony's neck if necessary to give you some control, then undo the throatlatch and noseband. Take the reins over his head, slip the headpiece over his ears and let the bit slide out of his mouth. Do everything slowly and gently so there is no risk of the pony jerking up his head and the bit getting caught.

Before you take off a saddle, run up the stirrups so they will not bang the pony's sides. Undo the girth and put it over the seat and lift off the saddle. The girth should be laid with the inside towards the leather; when you ride, the outside may get splashed with mud that could scratch the leather when dry.

sliding a saddle back into place

undoing a girth ~ with stirrups run up ~

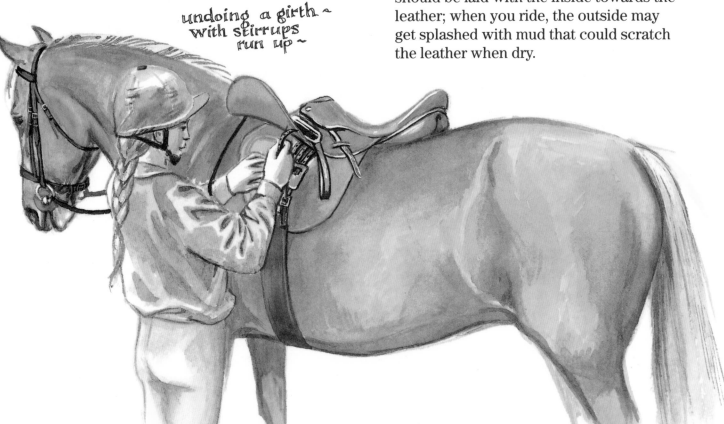

Bits and Pieces

eggbutt snaffle

bit-guard

loose-ring snaffle

There are many different sorts of bits and nosebands. Most riding school ponies wear snaffle bits, which are designed to be kind and suitable for novice riders to use. Always remember that a bit is only as kind – or as strong – as the hands at the end of the reins! The commonest kind of snaffle is the eggbutt snaffle, this has smooth sides to prevent it pinching the corners of the pony's mouth. It stays fairly still even if your hands move too much, which makes it a good bit for beginners to use.

Some ponies lean on an eggbutt snaffle and are happier, and easier to ride, in a loose ring snaffle. Because the rings move, they allow more play on the mouthpiece. This pony wears rubber bit-guards – rubber circles which fit on the bit between the rings and his face – to prevent his mouth being pinched.

A full cheek snaffle has bars down either side of the mouthpiece to help the rider steer. It is often used on young ponies to help them understand the rider's signals and on naughty ones to give the rider more control.

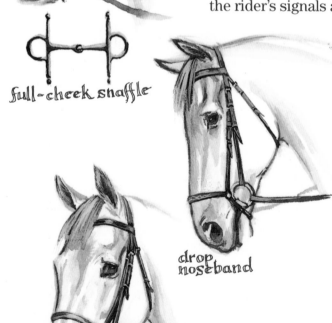

full-cheek snaffle

drop noseband

Cavesson

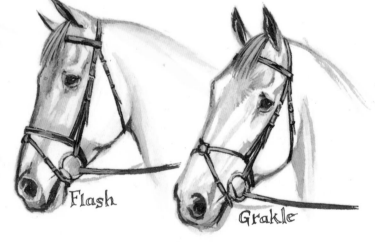

Flash

Grakle

Snaffle bridles usually have plain nosebands, called cavesson nosebands, but if the pony opens his mouth too much, he may be ridden in a drop, Flash or Grakle noseband to give the rider more control. It is important that these are not fastened too tightly; if they are so tight that the pony cannot move his jaw, he will be uncomfortable and fight the restriction.

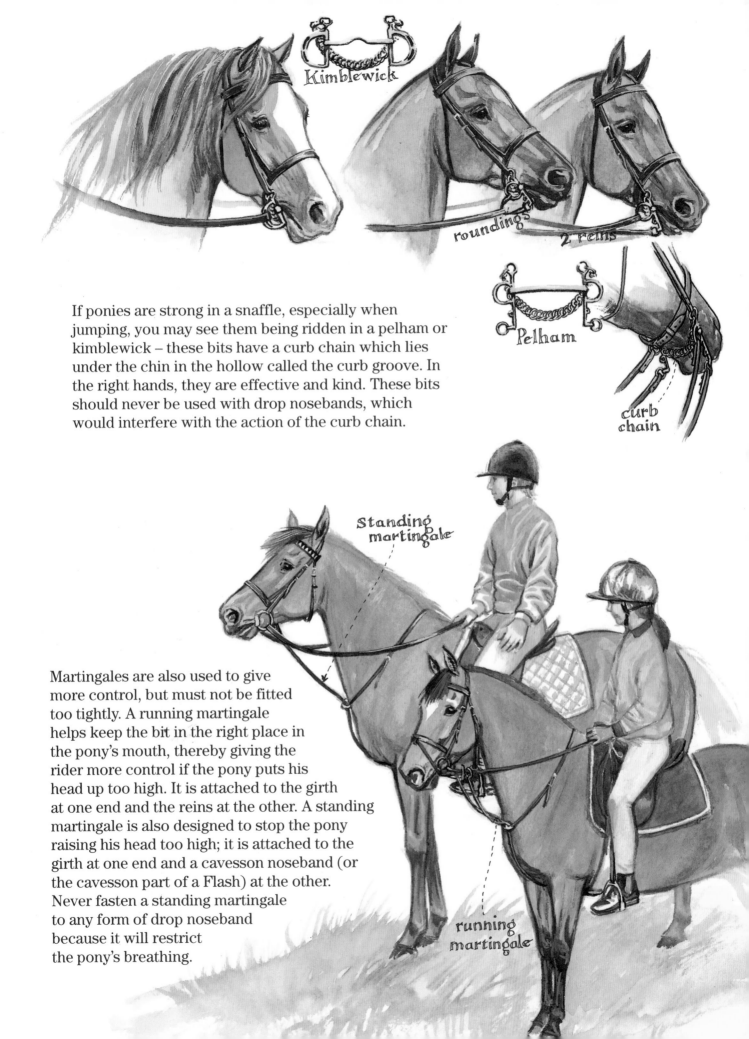

Kimblewick

rounding

2 reins

Pelham

curb chain

If ponies are strong in a snaffle, especially when jumping, you may see them being ridden in a pelham or kimblewick – these bits have a curb chain which lies under the chin in the hollow called the curb groove. In the right hands, they are effective and kind. These bits should never be used with drop nosebands, which would interfere with the action of the curb chain.

Standing martingale

Martingales are also used to give more control, but must not be fitted too tightly. A running martingale helps keep the bit in the right place in the pony's mouth, thereby giving the rider more control if the pony puts his head up too high. It is attached to the girth at one end and the reins at the other. A standing martingale is also designed to stop the pony raising his head too high; it is attached to the girth at one end and a cavesson noseband (or the cavesson part of a Flash) at the other. Never fasten a standing martingale to any form of drop noseband because it will restrict the pony's breathing.

running martingale

Bridles and Saddles

Your pony's saddle, bridle and bit must fit well. If they pinch or rub because they are too small or too large, the pony will be uncomfortable and will not be able to work properly. Imagine how you would feel if you had to wear shoes that were a size too big or too small! A badly fitting bit will make his mouth sore and a badly fitting saddle could damage his back. This pony's saddle is too big and will put weight on the wrong places. His bit is too large and too low in his mouth and will therefore bang against his teeth and the sides of his mouth. He may also put his tongue over the bit, which is uncomfortable for him and makes him difficult to control.

saddle too long and too large

bit too large and too low

checking the fitting of the throatlatch

This is a well-fitting bridle. The browband does not touch the base of the pony's ears and the noseband is fitted below the ends of the cheek bones so it does not rub them.

a well-fitting bit

A snaffle should be high enough to just wrinkle the corners of the pony's mouth. Bits come in different widths; the correct fitting allows for roughly a centimetre's gap between the cheekpiece and the pony's lips on each side. As a rough guide, an adult should be able to fit the width of a finger into this space on each side.

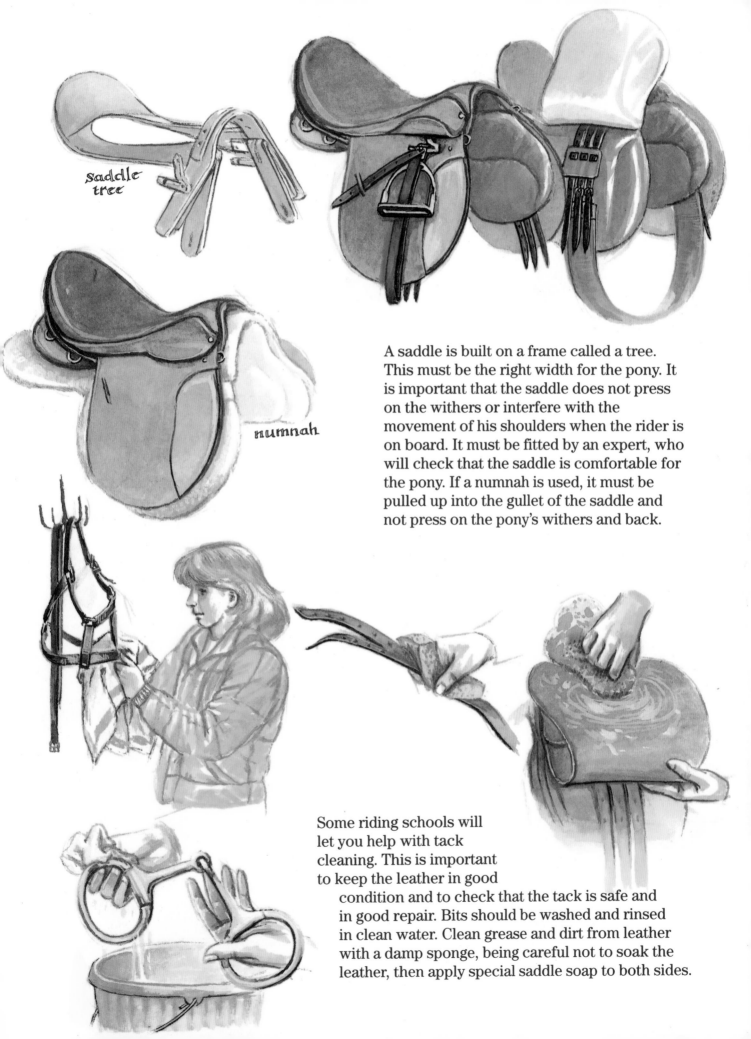

saddle tree

numnah

A saddle is built on a frame called a tree. This must be the right width for the pony. It is important that the saddle does not press on the withers or interfere with the movement of his shoulders when the rider is on board. It must be fitted by an expert, who will check that the saddle is comfortable for the pony. If a numnah is used, it must be pulled up into the gullet of the saddle and not press on the pony's withers and back.

Some riding schools will let you help with tack cleaning. This is important to keep the leather in good condition and to check that the tack is safe and in good repair. Bits should be washed and rinsed in clean water. Clean grease and dirt from leather with a damp sponge, being careful not to soak the leather, then apply special saddle soap to both sides.

Handlling Ponies

Handling ponies – catching, grooming and tacking up – will help you get to know them and understand their behaviour. People who understand ponies are often better riders, because they know what their reactions mean. Ponies give signals that show how they feel. For instance, a pony pricks his ears forward when he is interested in something and puts them back when he is frightened, uncomfortable or aggressive. A pony who lays back his ears when you tighten the girth is telling you that he is uncomfortable – either you are being rough, or his girth has been tightened roughly in the past. If he tries to nip you when you are tightening the girth from the ground, tie him up short enough to prevent him swinging his head round and adjust the girth slowly and gradually. If he is tacked up, take the reins over his head and pass them behind his neck, over the withers and back to your hand. You can then stop him turning his head to bite.

Many ponies blow out their stomachs when their girths are fastened. Check that it is tight enough to prevent the saddle slipping when you mount and check it again when you have ridden for a little while. To tighten the girth while mounted, keep your left foot in the stirrup and swing it in front of the saddle flap. Lift the flap, pull up the girth straps one at a time guiding the buckle prong – which is called a tongue – into the next hole with your fingers.

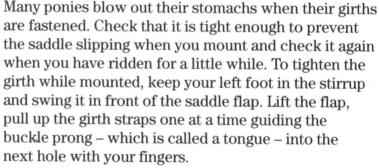

The length of your stirrup leathers can be altered from the ground or while you are mounted. If you are not sure of the length before you mount, fold your fingers and touch the knuckles to the stirrup bar where the leathers pass through. Stretch out your arm and run the stirrup leather along it – the bottom of the stirrup iron should reach your armpit. This gives you a rough idea and you can make a final adjustment from the saddle, if necessary.

Let your legs hang naturally round the pony's sides. If the stirrup iron is level with your ankle bone, the stirrups should be at a good working length for everyday riding and hacking. They should be shortened at least two holes for jumping.

To shorten or lengthen your stirrups from the saddle, keep your foot in the iron but lift your leg slightly away from the flap so your weight is not pressing down. Hold the free end of the leather and pull down so the buckle slides down from the bar. Move the buckle up or down and guide the tongue into the correct hole with your fingers. This takes practice – but eventually, as long as the stirrup leathers are supple and run freely, you should be able to do it without looking.

A good length of stirrup for everday riding ~ level with your ankle bone

Estimating the correct length of stirrup leathers from the ground

shortening stirrups from the saddle

Your instructor may ask you to carry a whip. Never use a wrist loop: if your whip has one of these, cut if off. If you put your hand through the loop and fall off the pony, you may hurt your wrist. Carry the whip so it rests across your thigh. Instructions for changing the whip from one hand to the other are given in the Jumping a Course section.

Leading and Grooming

Sometimes you will have to lead a pony. If he is wearing a headcollar, stand just in front of his shoulder and hold the rope in the hand nearest to him, about 20 cm (8 in) away from his face.

Hold the end of your rope in the other hand, but never wrap it round the hand in case he tries to break away and hurts you. Walk alongside him, looking ahead. Do not turn round and try to pull him along, because he will only pull back.

If he is tacked up, make sure the stirrup irons are run up the leathers so they do not flap about. Take the reins over his head and hold them in the same way as the leadrope. It is usual to lead from the nearside, though it is a good idea to practise from both sides in case you ever need to lead from the offside.

hoof pick

body brush

metal curry comb

sponges

hoof oil

fly repellent

rubber

dandy brush

rubber curry comb

water brush

cactus cloth

Grooming is important, not only to make the pony look nice but also because it enables you to check that he has not knocked or cut himself. Dried mud and dirt must be removed so it does not get trapped under his tack where it may rub and cause soreness and skin infections.

You may find all or some of these items in a grooming kit: hoof pick, stiff dandy brush, soft body brush, rubber and metal curry combs, separate sponges for eyes, nose and dock, stable rubber, water brush, hoof oil or dressing, fly repellent, cactus stain-removing cloth.

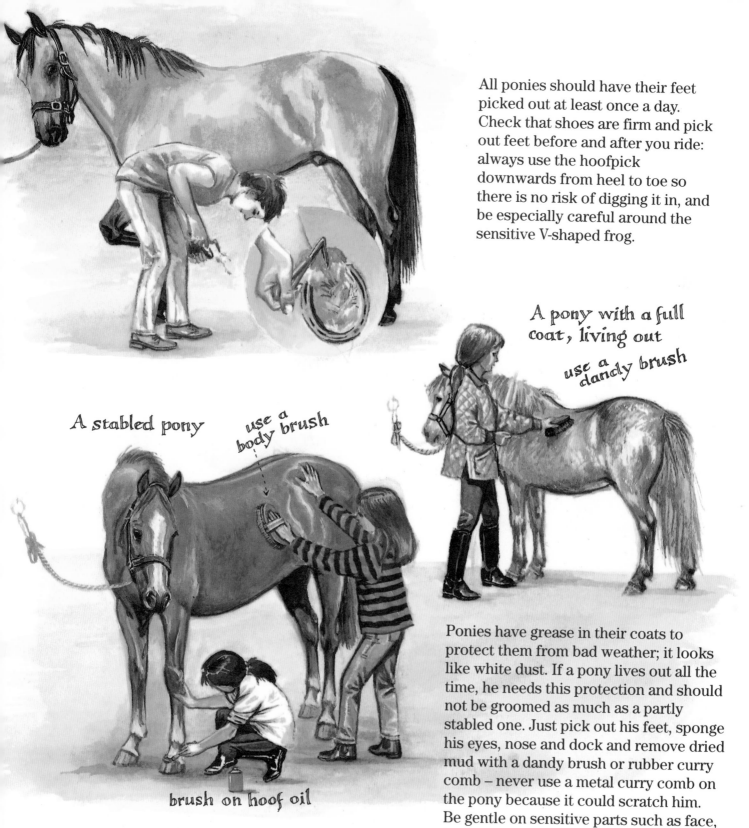

All ponies should have their feet picked out at least once a day. Check that shoes are firm and pick out feet before and after you ride: always use the hoofpick downwards from heel to toe so there is no risk of digging it in, and be especially careful around the sensitive V-shaped frog.

A pony with a full coat, living out

use a dandy brush

A stabled pony

use a body brush

brush on hoof oil

Ponies have grease in their coats to protect them from bad weather; it looks like white dust. If a pony lives out all the time, he needs this protection and should not be groomed as much as a partly stabled one. Just pick out his feet, sponge his eyes, nose and dock and remove dried mud with a dandy brush or rubber curry comb – never use a metal curry comb on the pony because it could scratch him. Be gentle on sensitive parts such as face, belly and legs: if necessary, use the flat of your hand.

Use a body brush to clean a stabled pony. Hold it in the hand nearest his body (left for nearside, right for offside) and use firm, short strokes. Every now and then, clean it on the curry comb and knock out the grease that is removed.

A slightly damp stable rubber puts a final finish on a coat and a damp water brush encourages the mane to lie flat ('laying a mane'). Hoof oil gives a finishing touch for special occasions.

Jumping

Learning to jump is an enjoyable part of learning to ride. All ponies can jump, but some enjoy it more and are better at it than others. The same applies to riders – some people are a little nervous about the idea of jumping, but there is no need to be. Your first jumps will be small and easy so that you can practise this new skill and your instructor will not ask you to do anything you cannot cope with safely and happily.

You have to change your riding position to stay in balance with your pony as he jumps. To make it easier, you should shorten your stirrups by at least two holes.

Your first jump will be simply a pole on the ground. Walk up to it and as the pony steps over, fold forwards from the hips, slide your hands forwards enough to give him freedom of his head and neck and look ahead, not at the ground.

shorter length for jumping

trotting poles

Approach the pole in a straight line, not at an angle (though when you are experienced and competing in a jump-off against the clock, you will learn how to jump at an angle to save time). A straight approach makes it easier for you and the pony to stay in balance. Your instructor may put down three or more poles in a row and ask you to trot through them. These are called trotting poles and help you to learn to keep the pony and yourself balanced and in control. They will be between 1.1 m (3 ft 6 in) and 1.4 m (4 ft 6 in) apart depending on the length of the pony's or horse's trot stride.

When you are happy with trotting poles, you will tackle your first proper jump. This will be two poles set to form a cross about 15 cm (6 in) high at the centre, perhaps with a pole on the ground to help the pony adjust his stride. This type of fence is called a cross pole and encourages the pony to jump in the centre, which is easiest for him and gives you a better chance of steering correctly for the next fence.

cross-pole

There are four parts to each jump – the approach, the take-off, the time in the air and the landing and getaway. Each is equally important and should be smooth and controlled, with no rushing or hesitating. At first you should jump from trot to give you more time to organise yourself; keep your trot calm but forward going, sit normally and look ahead. As the pony takes off, go forwards into your jumping position and when he lands, come gently back to your normal upright one. If you stay forwards all the time you will not be in a good position to tell him what you want to do next. He will probably canter when he lands; let him canter for two or three strides, then come quietly back to trot.

The next step is to jump two fences in a row, called a double. Your instructor should set them so that there is room for the pony to take one or two strides in between.

a double

Approach the first one in trot, just as you did your single fence; look ahead, sit up on landing and keep your legs round the pony's side and you should both take the second fence just as calmly and easily.

The same guidelines of keeping the pony straight, in control and in balance apply when you canter into a fence. It is important to have a nice rhythmic stride, because then the pony will arrive in the right place to take off easily. If he takes off too close or from too far away it is more difficult for him and he will be more likely to knock a fence down, or refuse or run out because he cannot manage to jump.

This section covers basic jumping. Later in this book you will find out about jumping a course and cross-country riding.

Making Progress

Riding in the school, jumping and hacking out will all be linked together to help you progress. With practice you will start to have more influence on the way your pony goes. Watch a good rider on a well-schooled pony and you will see that they both look confident and happy. The pony will move smoothly from one gait to another and will cope easily with turns and changes of directions, whether he is being ridden in the school or out in the open. This is what you should aim for.

Your pony must move in a purposeful but controlled way. He must feel as if he wants to get somewhere, but not as if he is rushing or pulling. This is what is meant by a pony 'going forwards' – if he is going forwards, he is more able to obey your instructions.

turning

You can now start to ask the pony to bend and turn in a more balanced way. To do this, you first have to work out which are the inside and outside aids. It is quite easy: your inside rein and leg are the ones nearest the centre of the turn and the outside ones are on the outside. So on the left rein, the inside rein is the left rein and your left leg is your inside leg. Think about asking for a slight bend to the inside as you go round corners. Use your inside leg on the girth and ask for a slight bend with the inside rein. Keep a contact on the outside rein, which is used to control the pony's speed, and slide your outside leg back a little to stop his quarters swinging out.

Always look ahead in the direction in which you want to go. Imagine that your pony is a train on a track and his legs are the wheels – the back ones must always follow the same path as the front ones to stay in balance.

back legs on same track as front

It may seem complicated at first, but gradually you will get the feel of what you are asking the pony to do. If you feel yourself becoming tense because you are trying so hard, stop for a moment: shrug your shoulders and relax, then take your feet out of the stirrups and stretch your legs.

shrugging

As you ride round the school, your instructor will tell you where to go. 'Go large' means ride right round the outside of the school; riding 'across the diagonal' means that you come round a corner and ride across the school to just before the corner diagonally opposite it.

going large around the school

turning from the corner to go across the diagonal

Schoolwork

Soon you will reach the stage where you and your pony are working as a team rather than you being just a passenger. The more you learn, the more fun riding will become. You can start to make your riding more accurate – to change direction and gait exactly when and where you want to. The best place to practise this is in an indoor or outdoor school, so you are riding in a set area. The school will probably have markers with letters on them round the edge; these are like signposts to tell you where to go. The letters used are A,K,E,H,C,M,B and F: strangely, no one knows what they stand for. You can remember them by saying 'All King Edward's Horses Can Manage Big Fences'. The letters are always in the same places and will probably be set round a 40 m by 20 m rectangle. This is the usual size for a schooling arena because it gives enough room for a pony, or horse, to work comfortably.

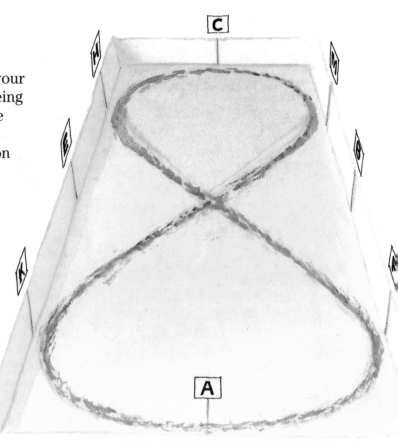

Your instructor may ask you to ride a 20 m circle starting and finishing at A, C, E or B.

A 20 m circle is easier for the pony to cope with than a smaller one and gives you time to ride accurately. You will also use the markers to change the diagonal across the school.

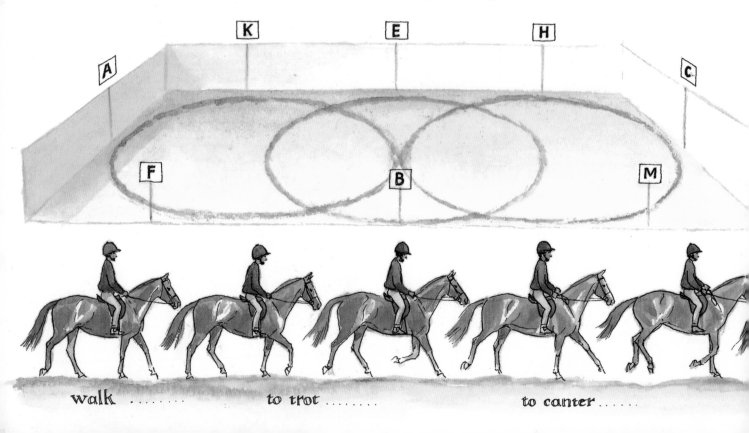

walk .... to trot .... to canter ......

Markers are also useful for making smooth changes of gait – for instance, you might be asked to trot down a long side of the school and go forwards to walk at A.

This means you have to start giving your aids at just the right time, which takes practice.

Halting at the centre of the school at X

K

E

A change of gait is called a transition. Think of it as changing gear rather than going faster or slower, that way the pony will stay in balance. You can make a transition from walk to trot, trot to canter, canter to trot and so on. Always think of riding forwards into a transition, even when you are changing from canter to trot, trot to walk or walk to halt so that the pony will change gear smoothly rather than jerkily.

Choose a letter (or a marker such as a tree along a bridlepath when you are out hacking) and see if you can make a transition there. You will find that you have to prepare for it a few strides before the marker: reorganise your balance, shorten your reins if necessary, close your legs round the pony's sides and ride forwards into your rein contact.

When you want him to make an upwards transition, such as walk to trot, ride forwards into the rein contact and allow with your hands as he goes forwards into the new gait. To make a downwards transition, such as trot to walk or walk to halt, close your legs round his sides and close your fingers on the reins without pulling back. As soon as he goes forwards to the new gait, or into halt, allow with your hands. Remember that as soon as he obeys your signals, you should stop giving them – if he obeys and you carry on asking, you will confuse him. If he does not obey, stop giving the signals for a couple of seconds and then ask again.

to trot . . . .   to walk . . . .   to halt

Problem Ponies

Ponies have moods, just like people, and sometimes you may have to cope with one who misbehaves. There are lots of reasons why a pony might be naughty – he could be getting too much to eat, he could be uncomfortable because his teeth are sharp or his tack does not fit, he could be frightened or he could simply be fed up! Your instructor should try to find the cause of the bad behaviour and correct the problem.

If a pony is lazy or ignores your aids, you must repeat them more strongly. Give him a chance to respond before asking again; if you carry on giving an aid while he is trying to obey, he will not understand what you want him to do. He should go forwards when you close your legs round his sides or perhaps give a slight nudge, but you should not have to kick him. Some ponies become so used to being kicked that they ignore it. If you give a light aid to start with, you can repeat it more firmly if the pony does not obey, but if you start with a strong aid such as a kick, you cannot reinforce it. Carry a whip with a lazy pony. If he does not respond to a slight leg aid, pause for a second and try a stronger one. If he still ignores you, give him a sharp tap with the whip just behind your leg. This is where a schooling whip is useful because it is longer than an ordinary one and you can use it without taking your hand off the reins.

holding a schooling whip

With a shorter whip, you must take your hand off the reins before using it or you will catch him in the mouth.

An excitable pony presents the opposite problem. He may jog, pull or buck. Excitable ponies should only be ridden by calm, competent riders who will not grow nervous and grab at the reins because this will only make things worse. Does a pony jog because he wants to catch up with another pony or because he always wants to be in front? Try riding in front, then alongside another and gradually fall back. Praise him when he walks calmly. If he starts to jog, say 'Walk' in a soothing voice. Some ponies settle if they are given a loose rein, others respond better to 'giving and taking' on the rein. You might have to experiment to find which works best.

checking a pony
between fences

bridging the
reins

Some ponies become strong when jumping or in company. Never set your hands in a continuous pull on the reins, again, 'give and take' works best. Remember that your legs should always be in contact with your pony's sides, even when he is pulling, so that you can keep him balanced. You need to sit fairly upright; if you lean forwards, you will find it hard to keep the pony in balance.

Bridging your reins helps you control a pony who becomes strong when cantering or galloping without pulling at his mouth. Jockeys often use this technique and it is just as effective on ponies!

If you think a pony is going to buck, sit upright and use your legs to push him forwards strongly. If he still bucks, it is sometimes easier to stay on if you can keep your weight slightly out of the saddle, because then the full force of the buck is not sent through your body.

Jumping a Course

Once you can stay in balance with your pony and are happy jumping small fences, you can try jumping a course. To ride well over jumps, you need to have the pony going well on the flat. If he is balanced and listening to your aids, he will cope with fences more easily. Never jump on your own, you need someone experienced with you to move poles, adjust distances between fences and help if anything goes wrong.

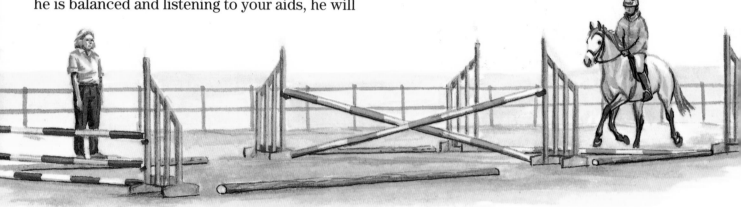

Your instructor will build lines of fences, called grids, to help you practise your jumping. They will be set up so that the pony has room to take one or two strides between each jump; the distances make it easy for him to take off and you can concentrate on correcting any mistakes in your riding. Common mistakes include leaning to one side or looking down as you approach the fence. Either will put your pony off balance and perhaps make him knock a fence down.

A good way of learning to jump a course is to start by putting poles on the ground, between jump wings, where your fences will be. Trot round over the poles and think about keeping your pony balanced and in a nice rhythm, making a straight approach to each pole and looking where you are going.

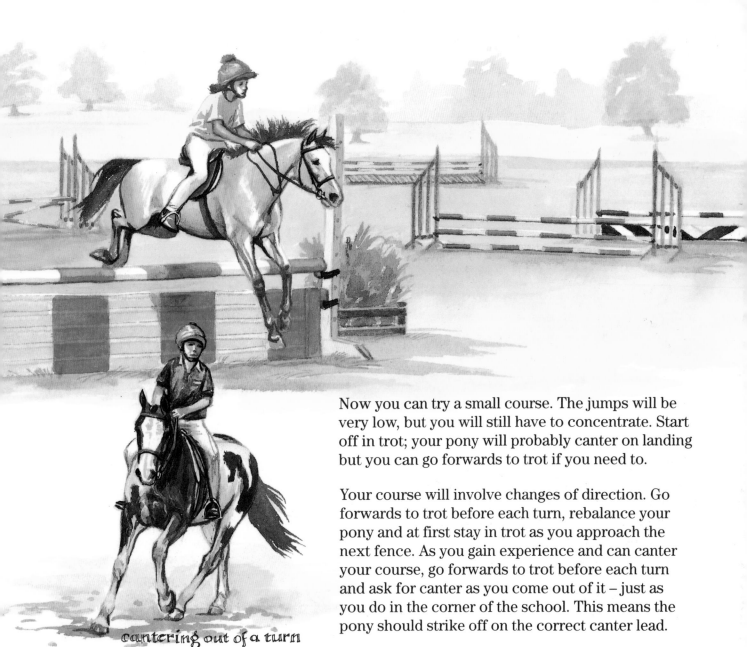

cantering out of a turn

Now you can try a small course. The jumps will be very low, but you will still have to concentrate. Start off in trot; your pony will probably canter on landing but you can go forwards to trot if you need to.

Your course will involve changes of direction. Go forwards to trot before each turn, rebalance your pony and at first stay in trot as you approach the next fence. As you gain experience and can canter your course, go forwards to trot before each turn and ask for canter as you come out of it – just as you do in the corner of the school. This means the pony should strike off on the correct canter lead.

You need to be able to change a whip from one hand to the other both on the flat and when jumping. The whip is a back-up to your leg aids. If you approach a jump carrying the whip in your right hand and the pony runs out to the left, change the whip to your left hand – and if necessary apply it behind the girth – on your next approach. To change a whip from your right hand to your left one, hold both reins in your right hand and put your left hand on the whip handle, below the right one and with the fingers pointing towards you. Turn the whip over the pony's withers and let it rest on your thigh.

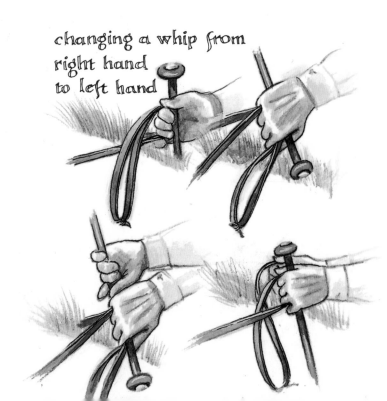

changing a whip from right hand to left hand

Cross Country

Jumping cross-country fences is fun for rider and pony. You will need all the skills you have built up through riding on the flat, through grids and round small courses. Cross-country courses are much longer than show-jumping ones and have bigger gaps between the fences. They are ridden at a faster pace, but still in rhythm and balance, though some fences may still need to be ridden from trot or a slow, bouncy canter. There are lots of types of cross-country fence; your instructor will start you over easy ones such as small logs.

Safety is important. This rider wears a skull cap and body protector, which some people also prefer to wear for show jumping. The pony wears brushing boots and overreach boots to protect his legs; they must be fitted carefully so they do not pinch or rub.

It is a good idea to tie a knot at the end of your reins. If your pony stumbles and you drop the reins, or if you need to let them out to their full length to give him the maximum freedom, they will not fall down his neck and there is no risk of him putting a foot through them and slipping.

A bounce fence has two parts which the pony has to jump without taking a stride in between, i.e. he lands then takes off again straight away. It needs a controlled, bouncy approach. Your instructor might introduce you to this sort of fence by setting up a bounce of two small cross poles.

Ditches should be approached in a bouncy trot or canter. Keep your approach straight and rhythmical and look ahead, not down at the ditch. This ditch is part of a coffin complex – two fences with a ditch in the middle.

Most cross-country courses have water jumps. At first you will simply have to ride through it: later on you might jump small fences into and out of water. If you go into water too fast your pony will find it hard to stay balanced, so keep your approach straight, controlled and bouncy. It is usually best to go through in trot.

British Library Cataloguing in Publication Data
A catalogue record for this book is available from the British Library.

ISBN 0.85131.608.5

Published in Great Britain in 1994 by
J.A. Allen & Company Ltd.,
1, Lower Grosvenor Place, Buckingham Palace Road,
London, SW1W 0EL.

Typeset in Great Britain by Textype Typesetters
Printed in Hong Kong by Dah Hua Printing Press Co. Ltd.
Colour scanned in Hong Kong by Tenon & Polert Colour Scanning Ltd.